W9-DDX-521

WHOSE TOES ARE THOSE?

JOANNE RANDOLPH

PowerKiDS
press™

New York

Published in 2009 by The Rosen Publishing Group, Inc.
29 East 21st Street, New York, NY 10010

First Edition

Book Design: Julio Gil
Photo Researcher: Jessica Gerweck

Photo Credits: Cover, pp. 5, 7, 11, 13, 15, 17, 19, 24 (top right, bottom) Shutterstock.com; pp. 9, 23 © SuperStock, Inc.; p. 21, 24 (top left) © Roland Seitre/Peter Arnold Inc.

Library of Congress Cataloging-in-Publication Data

Randolph, Joanne.
  Whose toes are those? / Joanne Randolph. — 1st ed.
      p. cm. — (Animal clues)
  Includes index.
  ISBN 978-1-4042-4452-8 (library binding)
  1. Foot—Juvenile literature. I. Title.
  QL950.7.R36 2009
  590—dc22
                                                    2007048206

Manufactured in the United States of America

CONTENTS

What has three black **pads** on its furry toes?

This lion cub has three black pads on its furry toes.

Who has three orange toes on each **webbed** foot?

A duck has three orange toes on each webbed foot.

Whose toes are sticky and help it climb trees?

This tree frog's sticky toes help it climb trees.

Who belongs to these big, round toes?

17

An elephant belongs to these big, round toes.

Who has three toes with very long **claws**?

A slow-moving sloth has three toes with long claws.

WORDS TO KNOW

claws

pads

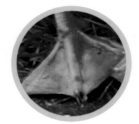

webbed

WEB SITES

Due to the changing nature of Internet links, PowerKids Press has developed an online list of Web sites related to the subject of this book. This site is updated regularly. Please use this link to access the list:
www.powerkidslinks.com/acl/toes/

24